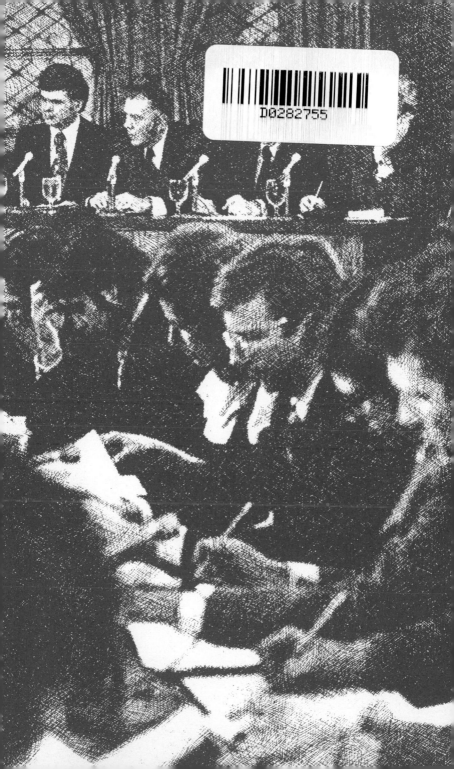

Can Congress Control Spending?

A Town Hall Meeting on Domestic Affairs
sponsored by the American Enterprise Institute
held at
American Enterprise Institute
Washington, D.C.

March 6, 1973

Robert Goralski
Moderator

Can Congress Control Spending?

William Proxmire

Al Ullman
John W. Byrnes
Paul W. McCracken
Charles L. Schultze

Town Hall Meeting

American Enterprise Institute for Public Policy Research
Washington, D.C.

Foreword

In a free society, public attitudes are crucial for public policy formation. They define the range of options open to public officials in coping with the major issues of the day. It is vital, therefore, that those who help form public attitudes have available the results of research, analysis, and innovative thought from as wide a range of sources as possible.

Partisan controversy over such issues as inflation, health care, taxation, women's rights, and public spending will, of course, continue to make its contribution to this end. Dedicated to nonpartisan policy research, the American Enterprise Institute can approach issues in a different, but no less effective, manner. This approach is exemplified in AEI's Town Hall Meetings on Domestic Policy.

The format for this series is designed to encourage dialogue, that form of human communication that provokes intelligent exchange of ideas rather than harangue. Each meeting opens with the presentation of papers by the principals, the first and longest of which sets the stage for the subsequent discussion. After the formal presentations, there is an exchange of views among the principals, followed by questions and comments from a group of experts. The proceedings are made available to the public in books such as this, as well as in video and audio cassettes and in films.

By emphasizing thoughtful conversation in the arena of national policy formation, the American Enterprise Institute hopes to add a new dimension to the reasoned consideration of the questions now being raised about America's future. We believe that, in the process, it will become evident that Lord Keynes was right—that, indeed, "the power of vested interests is vastly exaggerated compared with the gradual encroachment of ideas."

William J. Baroody
President
American Enterprise Institute
for Public Policy Research

Contents

Part 1

Congress <u>Can</u> Control
Spending

William Proxmire

What is the answer to the question, can Congress control spending? Before that question can be answered yes or no, we must address ourselves to a number of more specific considerations and questions.

Background

Current year's spending is a presidential prerogative. The first point is that "spending" or "outlays" for any particular year are peculiarly the province of the President. The $268.7 billion President Nixon has proposed to spend in fiscal year 1974 is made up of numerous items, and Congress cannot exercise control over more than about half of them this year. Let me be specific.

Some $82 billion in the budget comes from the social security trust fund. Another $4 to $5 billion is in the highway trust fund. Interest on the debt accounts for about $25 billion more. Congress—and, for the most part, the President too—has virtually no control *this year* over either the collection or spending of these funds. That is a function of the past. In this respect these funds are largely "uncontrollable."

Appropriations are not outlays. There is another way to look at it, too. Of the total of $268.7 billion in the proposed budget, only about $157 billion or 58 percent is money which Congress will appropriate this year. And most of that amount will be for wages and salaries. The rest of the money that Congress will appropriate—the other $46 billion or so—will not be spent for years into the future.

How far into the future? In the case of urban renewal, the average length of time between appropriation and spending is seven to nine years. In the case of a weapons system, the average is three to four years. And similar lags occur for public works, buildings, water and sewer, housing, and other projects. In fact, there is a rule of thumb we use in the appropriations committee that to cut $1 from this year's budget, we must cut $3 from appropriations and, conversely, to increase spending by $1, we must increase appropriations by $3.

$300 billion backlog. To put it yet another way, much of what will be spent in fiscal 1974—about $110 billion—will come from the backlog of $298 billion in federal funds which the President has at his disposal. And much of what Congress appropriates this year will go into a new backlog which will not be spent for years into the future. In fact, the estimate is that at the end of the 1974 fiscal year, the backlog will be $305.7 billion, or $7 billion more than at the beginning of the year.

So how can Congress control spending when so much of it is made up of funds appropriated in the past or trust funds over which Congress has no immediate control, and is expended for interest on the debt, which varies with economic conditions, and for required payments for items like the Commodity Credit Corporation where the secretary of Agriculture pays the bills first and submits the amount to Congress as an accomplished fact?

The budget establishes the President's priorities. Before answering that question, let me ask another. Does the President control the current year's budget to any significant extent? The answer, I think, is yes. To the degree that the budget is "controllable" this year, it is the President who controls it. The budget document states, really, the President's priorities or decisions for spending. He chooses them. To the degree that anyone can determine the rate and pace of spending, it is he.

While one can argue against the impounding of funds—especially when it is done on grounds that the President just does not like a particular program—the fact is that every year the President makes a judgment as to whether urban renewal spending shall be, say, $900 million or $1.2 billion, whether the Defense Department can spend $75 or $81 billion, or whether the Corps of Engineers will spend $1.3 or $1.6 billion for public works. In this respect, it is the President and not Congress who is responsible for spending levels. And this year, in my judgment, the President had enough flexibility to establish an outlay figure anywhere from $235 billion to $290 billion, instead of the $268.7 billion which he has proposed.

Ways to Control Spending

1. Impose a ceiling on presidential prerogatives. In spite of all this, the first part of my answer to the question—can Congress control spending?—is yes. Congress *can* control spending and it can do so this year. But it can control spending this year in only one way. That way is to do exactly what the President has repeatedly asked it to do and impose a ceiling on the amount the President can spend, a ceiling on outlays.

Some members of Congress have opposed this with great vehemence. They call it a usurpation of their power. I think they could not be more wrong. A ceiling does not limit congressional control. Actually it limits the President's ability to spend because, in the absence of a ceiling, he has leeway. This year, as I pointed out, he could have reached into the backlog and come up with even more than $269 billion.

I have proposed that the Congress establish a spending or outlay ceiling for fiscal year 1974 at $265 billion. This figure is $4 billion below the President's proposed level of spending.

In my view the President's budget is too high. He proposes to spend $268.7 billion. This is $19 billion or 7.5 percent more than we spent in fiscal 1973. It is $22 billion or 9 percent more than the $246 billion originally proposed for that year. This is one of the biggest increases in the peacetime history of our country. Given the rampaging inflation at home, the devaluation of the dollar abroad, and the fat and waste which one can find by any intelligent examination of the budget of any department or any agency in the government, that is too much and should be cut.

2. Reform the procedures of Congress. The second thing Congress must do so that it can control spending is to reform its own procedures. We are now in the process of doing that, both through the tentative proposals of the Joint Study Committee on the Budget and through numerous individual bills introduced by a number of House and Senate members. Unfortunately, these measures will not be effective until next year at the earliest.

In my view, here is what Congress must do:

Establish category ceilings. First, as I have said, we must establish an annual overall spending or outlay ceiling. Within that overall ceiling, we should establish ceilings on a category-by-category basis—for defense, housing, space, agriculture, and so forth. This must be done every year and must be done *early* every year, long before July 1st when the new fiscal year begins.

Control the backlog. Second, we should reduce and control the $298 billion backlog so that it cannot be used to thwart congressional intentions. Let me illustrate.

In fiscal years 1968 through 1972, Congress cut the President's requests for defense spending by $18.4 billion, including supplementals. During that same period, the Pentagon not only did not cut spending but it actually spent $22 billion more than Congress had appropriated and $3 billion more than the President had requested. Now how did it do that? Every time we cut defense appropriations, the Pentagon dipped into its $40 billion backlog and made up the cuts. So year after year outlays were what the Pentagon said they would be, no matter how much Congress cut.

The conclusion I come to is that if Congress wants to control spending it must reduce the backlog and limit appropriations severely to one- and two-year funds.

Stop reprogrammings. Third, Congress should refuse to reprogram funds. Routinely agencies come to the chairman of a House or Senate appropriations subcommittee to say, We have a shortage of funds for Project A and an excess of funds for Project B, so please let's spend Project B funds for Project A this year. It was through this device that the Cheyenne helicopter, one of the biggest weapons-system lemons yet devised, was funded even after it had been stopped.

Congress should not only refuse reprogrammings but the Office of Management and Budget (OMB), which I understand does not now review reprogrammings, should get on top of this major leak in government spending that has so distorted our priorities. Neither individual agencies nor individual chairmen of the House or Senate committees should be allowed to act, either on behalf of the administration or on behalf of the entire Congress. Too often they are in league with each other to spend money.

Limit supplementals to true emergencies. Fourth, we should limit supplemental appropriations bills to truly emergency needs instead of appeals from previous actions, as is too often the case now.

Last year, for example, the Department of Housing and Urban Development (HUD) came in for a $250 million urban renewal supplemental appropriation which it said would be spent under the regular urban renewal program. I opposed the request on grounds that the money would not be spent for years into the future. HUD called it an emergency—although it would take years to obligate the money, let alone spend it.

But the administration and HUD demanded it—albeit a few weeks before the election—and they got it. There was one quarter of a billion dollars which Congress appropriated at the administration's insistence, thus committing us to big spending many years into the future.

Require more than illustrative budgets. Fifth, we should do away with "illustrative budgets" and demand specific line-item appropriations for every major project.

What do I mean by illustrative budgets? The main example of this kind of thing is the foreign aid budget. The U.S. Agency for International Development (AID) is given a pot of money from which to draw. AID's representations to Congress of what country is to get what amount are merely "illustrative." It is not held to them at all but can shift funds any way it wishes. This removes congressional control over the funds for specific countries and allows the agency to do almost entirely what it pleases.

Through this device, plus the use of the backlog (that is, diverting funds from the defense budget), North Vietnam just may get billions without congressional approval.

Include "tax expenditures." Sixth, we must begin to require that the budget include each agency's "tax expenditures." HUD's budget, for example, is given as $3 to $4 billion. But that is only part of it, and the smaller part at that. Another $6 to $7 billion goes to housing each year through tax subsidies and revolving funds. If any intelligent judgment is to be made about the size and effectiveness of housing expenditures, these should be shown clearly in HUD's budget.

Control the "uncontrollables." Seventh, we should find means of controlling the "uncontrollables." The uncontrollability of an expenditure is really a function of time. For example, the $20 billion in Pentagon procurement is called an "uncontrollable" item. But is this really uncontrollable? Billions could be saved through procurement reform and tough oversight. And Medicare is considered an "uncontrollable," but administrative changes effected by Senate Finance Committee oversight hearings brought major savings. We must find ways, preferably through regular committee oversight hearings, to control the uncontrollables.

Examine formula grants. Eighth, the same procedure of committee oversight hearings, along with changes in the basic law, should be to examine the so-called formula grants. In the case of these grants, Congress can control the long-run total to some degree, but has no control over the details.

Provide staff. Ninth, Congress urgently needs an adequate

professional staff. At the present time, for example, as chairman of the Subcommittee on HUD, Space, Science, and Veterans of the Appropriations Committee, I have only one full-time staff man available to me. And this subcommittee handles appropriations of $20 billion. Without staff, we are far too dependent on the particular agencies for facts and arguments.

Establish adversary proceedings. Tenth, and in a sense perhaps most important of all, we should establish adversary proceedings instead of the current ex parte hearings where routinely only those asking for the funds appear and snow the Congress. They are biased to conserve or build their empires, and they never ask for less. A veteran of the appropriations committee staff, a man who has served the committee for twenty-six years, told me that not one committee witness in a thousand calls for spending reductions. The agencies are the source for both the facts and the arguments that we hear. Is it any wonder that federal spending is exploding?

These are the answers to the question: can Congress control the budget? Yes, we can, *if* we establish an annual ceiling on outlays and *if* we reform our procedures.

Part 2

Commentaries

Al Ullman

Senator Proxmire has presented us with an excellent summary of how to tighten numerous nuts and bolts in the appropriations process. The senator and I are both members of the Joint Study Committee on Budget Control, to which he referred several times, and just today this committee began public hearings on this issue.

The basic thrust of what the committee is trying to accomplish is to tie the revenue and spending functions together, both in the House and Senate, and in this way see to it that all expenditures are considered only in the context of conflicting priorities and within an overall spending framework. We would do this by establishing separate committees on the budget in the House and the Senate, but with a joint staff for the two committees.

The House committee would meet at the beginning of each session of Congress and determine the proper level of expenditures and budget authority for the coming fiscal year —after fully considering the fiscal, monetary and other economic factors involved. At the same time, this committee would determine the appropriate revenue and debt levels. The expenditure total would, as Senator Proxmire indicated, be allocated on a major program basis. These limitations would be included in a resolution acted upon by the House, then considered by the Senate budget committee, and acted upon by the Senate. Any differences would be ironed out in conference.

The expenditure and obligational ceiling would be set early in each Congress, before appropriation bills were considered and before backdoor spending measures were reported out of any of the other committees. It would be necessary to apply the ceiling to *all* spending measures, since at present only

44 percent of total spending goes through the appropriations committees.

I believe that, each year, when this resolution reached the floor of the House and the Senate, we would have a major budget debate—something unique in U.S. political experience, but traditional in some other countries, such as Great Britain and Canada, and in many of our state legislatures. When this budget debate occurs, I would want all of the members of the House to have a clear chance to act on the expenditure ceiling—and on the priority allocations as well. But equally important, we should insist that if a member wants an expenditure increase in one category, he should provide for an expenditure reduction in another category— or alternatively, raise the ceiling and admit that he wants to increase the spending total. This is something we have never done, and it is what we mean by facing up to the priority decisions in Congress.

Some have said that Congress does not know enough about the budget early in the session to make these meaningful priority decisions at that time. The committee expects to deal with this problem by providing Congress with a second chance, an opportunity in the latter part of each congressional session to reconsider the expenditure ceiling and revenue decisions previously made.

If the Congress can establish a mechanism to set revenue goals and expenditure ceilings and if it can project its own priorities within that framework—in other words, fit the parts into the whole—then the issue of impoundment will fade away.

Despite the implications of the current wrangle over the budget, I believe the fundamental task is to establish a workable, long-range mechanism to enable Congress to come to terms with the hard realities of budgeting. Last year, when I authored an amendment to create a budget committee, I felt the time was right to create a legislative budget, as opposed to a presidential budget, so that Congress could reassert its basic constitutional prerogatives. I feel even more strongly that the time is right today. Judging from the interest and response of everyone on the study committee, we are off to a good start.

I am convinced that we will only be able to control spending, and control it rationally, if the members of Congress are able to evaluate it in a framework of alternative national goals. This is the real challenge, and the key to the solutions we all seek.

John W. Byrnes

I think we must generally agree with Senator Proxmire's premise that, under the present situation, it is the President who controls spending. Thank heaven he is, because Congress has certainly forfeited control. If the President were not exercising strong control, we would be in a real mess. It is regrettable, therefore, that there are so many voices in the Congress condemning the President for stepping into the breach. Instead of fighting his efforts, they should be applauding them.

There is no question that Congress has the power to control spending if it has the will to do so. After all, it has absolute authority over revenues and spending; not one penny can be spent unless authorized and appropriated by the Congress. The difficulty is that Congress has been authorizing and appropriating with an abandon that is far beyond our capacity or our willingness to finance—except through borrowing. Spending is out of control.

What we are really talking about is how to establish a sound and rational fiscal policy—one that determines revenue and expenditure levels for each year consistent with the needs of the country, economically and socially. We are talking about controlling both the level of spending in any particular year and the distribution of that spending among the various government programs—the establishment of priorities. Only in this way can we control *future* spending.

The trouble is that Congress never addresses itself to this point. By its failure to do so, it has abandoned its authority and abdicated its responsibility.

Congress authorizes expenditure, generally on an openended basis and for an indefinite period. Then, in the appropriation process, it addresses itself not to the level of spending in any particular year but, as the senator has pointed out, to obligational authority, the right to spend a given amount over an indefinite period of time. The President submits an expenditure budget for the coming fiscal year, and congressmen make speeches about it, but the Congress itself all but ignores it. The Congress goes to work not on the expenditure levels for the particular year, but on the budget of obligational authority—primarily the new obligational authority requested by the President. The senator referred to this anomaly, and I think it needs emphasis.

We read today, for example, about the expenditure budget of $268 billion for fiscal year 1974, but the budget of new obligational authority requested by the President totals $288 billion. And there will be appropriations (authority to spend) left over from prior years of $298 billion. If the Congress gives the President the new authority requested in this year's budget, he will have total spending authority as we begin the 1974 fiscal year of $586 billion. And it is he who will decide the rate at which this will be spent and when it will be spent.

So the very first thing Congress must do is restructure the legislative process so that it *does* address itself to the level and rate of spending on a yearly basis. It must address itself to the budget of expenditures.

Senator Proxmire recommends, and I agree, that Congress should establish an annual spending ceiling. I think I fought as hard as anybody a year ago to get that ceiling established, to write it into law. This is the least Congress should do. But Congress refused, despite the President's urgent request. A ceiling was vehemently opposed by the majority leadership in the Congress and it failed to get majority support.

The second big problem is that congressional procedures never address themselves to budget totals, or to the effect of the separate actions in the totals. The total is like Topsy, it just grows. Authorizations flow from some 300 congressional committees and subcommittees, each having a particular sympathy and allegiance to the governmental activity under its relatively narrow jurisdiction. For all intents and purposes, none of these committees has any exposure to the overall fiscal requirements and relative importance and needs of other programs outside its jurisdiction. Then the appropriations process takes over, and it is equally self-centered. Numerous appropriations subcommittees concern themselves with only a segment of the budget, never with the total.

The total budget is no less than the sum of all its parts. A way must be found to ensure that, in the process of authorizing and appropriating funds, the funds sought for the various segments are balanced against each other and then against a potential total. There must be a limitation in terms of the needs of society and the economy.

Congress must develop a system for establishing priorities. This task, in my judgment, will probably be the most difficult. It will be difficult not just because it requires some fundamental changes in procedures, but because it means that each of the numerous committees that now has an input will have to surrender some of the authority it now enjoys. No chairman or committee will do this without a struggle.

It will also be difficult because somewhere and somehow some group in the Congress must have the authority—but, more important, the *guts*—to say no, and then the majority in the Congress must accept that decision. When we realize that we are talking about an institution of 535 elected representatives, all with individual viewpoints and philosophies, we can conclude that this is not going to be an easy task.

It seems to me that more important than all the suggested structural changes is the general attitude within the Congress and on the part of the public. However complete the structural changes, however clear the definition of what should be done, it will all be meaningless unless there is a serious determination to pursue a realistic, sound fiscal policy, regardless of the political pressures. There must be a willingness to "bite the bullet." I know from experience that one of the most difficult things for a congressman or a senator to do is to say no to a group seeking funds for a project that, from its narrower point of view, is both desirable and essential. It's real tough. But if we are to get control, everybody's pet project cannot be funded. Some must go by the wayside, some must be deferred.

This brings me to the final and probably the most important point that I would make. The demand and support for spending control must come from the majority of the American people. It is eminently unfair to blame the Congress or the President for runaway spending or high taxes if, individually or in groups, voters continue to ask for more government service with no regard to cost or relative priority. We the people must curb our appetite. We must stop asking for services that we are unwilling to pay for. Too many people overlook the fact that there is a "me" in economy. Yes, and we must give positive support, it seems to me, to those in government who are sincerely trying to keep spending within bounds.

I was in the Congress quite a while. I saw many monuments erected to special groups or by special groups to congressmen who were advocates of full and generally excessive funding of their particular projects. The yes-men have their walls lined with plaques attesting to their great work for one cause or another. It is time to erect monuments to those in the Congress who have the guts to say *"no."*

Paul W. McCracken

Senator Proxmire stated that the President's budget for fiscal 1974 is too high, and it ought to be reduced. A lot of people, probably the majority of the citizenry, would agree. Although I do not speak for the President, he also might agree that a $265 billion budget for next year, up $15 billion over last year, ought to be enough.

The reason for public concern about the relentlessness of this tendency for the budget to rise rapidly is no mystery. It can be found in the budget facts themselves. Last year, government outlays (federal, state, and local) were equal to almost 40 percent of national income and the *rise* in these outlays during the last five years has been equal to about 46 percent of the *rise* in national income. If national defense outlays are omitted, the figure is almost 45 percent. It is not surprising, therefore, that concern about the processes that determine the aggregate volume of public spending has been mounting. People who have strong aspirations to improve further their own material levels of living apparently regard this as an overly generous sharing of their incomes with the government.

Yet the budget is where it is. The process that produces these decisions is giving us a $250 billion federal budget this year and a projected $265 to $270 billion budget for 1974, and the pressures are extremely strong to push the total even higher. We seem to be at a historical confrontation between a budget expanding relentlessly and rapidly and a citizenry increasingly concerned about the large proportion of increases in the national income that are being absorbed by government.

The first step toward realism is not to delude ourselves that the problem is simply waste in spending. There are inefficiencies in the Congress, in the executive branch, in universities, and in other organizations of society, and waste is, of course, never to be condoned. The budget problem, however, is far more fundamental than waste. It reflects two things that are related. One is the fact that for governments, or businesses, or families, the aggregate of ideas for spending money which, looked at individually, seem meritorious will always add to more than any viable total. In that sense, government budgets and family budgets reflect the same basic problem. (In some other respects there are, of course, differences.)

The budget problem also reflects the fact that a strongly organized interest group can focus a pressure on the Congress (and on government generally) which is far stronger than the group's numbers would imply. This tends to produce an upward bias in the total relative to what the diffused general interest would really prefer. This is particularly true since, as the senator has pointed out, the Congress acts on appropriations, not outlays. A leading item in Washington's lexicon of overworked sentences surely must be, "It would add only a few million to outlays this year."

There is, I believe, a growing measure of agreement that congressional decision-making procedures must include some way by which the Congress can focus on and accept responsibility for total outlays. The procedure must enable it to evaluate not only whether a proposed expenditure looks *good* but whether it looks good *enough* to out-compete other proposals, also promising in their own right, for space within a limited total.

The answer is not, however, simply to impose a spending ceiling on the President. As my colleagues tonight have indicated, a ceiling amounts to dumping the hot potato of making the tough decisions, each of which arouses some interest group's ire, on the President. In the short run, it may be tempting. In the longer run, responsibilities evaded are always rights and prerogatives eroded. This would be a good recipe for achieving further abdication of congressional prerogatives for decisions about national priorities. It would not give us good budget policies. But, more fundamentally, such atrophy of the congressional role would signal an ominous deterioration of the quality of our national government.

Senator Proxmire's proposals for congressional approval of not only a total but also subtotals for broad functional categories, therefore, strike me as sound. This must be coupled, however, with far better procedures for evaluating the spending path for future years down which program decisions for "this year" are leading us.

My answer to the question of whether Congress can control spending is in the affirmative because any other answer is unthinkable. What is involved is not only good budgetry. It is also a reassertion of the basic prerogatives, roles and responsibilities of the Congress that are so important to our structure and system of government.

Charles L. Schultze

Let me start with a slightly different emphasis, namely, that the problem of government is not to see how little can be spent, any more than it is to see how little can be spent on housing or on investment or on anything else. The problem is the right amount of spending for the right things. People, of course, disagree both on what is the right amount and what are the right things.

Essentially the proper approach to controlling spending is to make sure that what the government spends reflects in some sense a conscious decision that that is really what we want to spend and that is what we want to spend for various things—defense, urban renewal, education, and the like. We want to make sure that spending does not grow like Topsy and that we are not captives of the past.

This introduces the first problem in controlling government spending. As Senator Proxmire has stressed, but I would like to stress it even more, the President has much flexibility in determining the actual amount to be spent in a given year because he has a large backlog of spending authorizations which the Congress has enacted in prior years. But, as a matter of fact, both the President and the Congress are captives of the past when it comes to spending.

Let me illustrate this point. What will be spent in the coming fiscal year on an F-14 Navy plane has practically nothing to do with any decisions anybody in the federal government is going to make in that year; rather it is determined by contracts let for those planes one, two, or three years ago. What will be spent on urban renewal in the coming fiscal year—the checks that the federal government will write for this purpose—has nothing to do with any decisions anybody is going to make about urban renewal; rather it is mostly the result of commitments and urban renewal grants made to local communities two, three, four, and five years ago, and which those communities are now cashing in as the contractors gradually get the work done. Similarly, this year the Congress may vote $100 million for nuclear reactors for a new nuclear aircraft carrier. Only $100 million. But that action would result in $2 billion worth of spending over future years—for the ship, for the planes on the deck, and for the escorts to go around the ship.

The moral of this story is that the spending in 1974 is very heavily determined by decisions made three, four, and five years ago and, conversely, that the decisions made in 1974 about all sorts of government programs will partly affect what we spend in 1974, but very heavily affect what we spend in 1975, 1976, and 1977.

The analogy of the average family is appropriate. If I were to ask what you are going to spend next year, your answer would be determined only in part by the decisions you make about spending next year. It would be heavily determined by the mortgage you entered into on a house several years ago, the car you bought on an installment contract one year ago, and the items you put on charge accounts and are now paying off.

Therefore, in order to control spending—in the sense of not just trying to keep it as small as possible but also trying to get human decisions so that we determine our own fate— it is essential that we look ahead. It is essential that we look at the impact of this year's spending decisions on the years ahead.

This means the following:

First, the executive should be required to submit to the Congress a budget which spells out in detail the fiscal consequences in 1974, 1975, and 1976 of its current proposals— not just how those proposals will affect spending next year, but how they will affect it down the road. The present administration is to be congratulated because it has begun to do this. But it has not yet submitted the information in enough detail to give Congress the kind of control it needs.

Second, every congressional action that requires or leads to spending should be accompanied by an explicit report which documents what that will mean for spending two, three, and four years into the future.

Third, some congressional committee—the Joint Economic Committee, the appropriations committee, or some new committee—should be charged with periodically updating those longer-range forecasts so that the Congress and the public will always know what the future consequences of current actions will be.

Now let me turn to another part of the problem. It is fairly easy—and fairly dangerous—for the Congress to do nothing more than devise a procedure to set a spending ceiling. It is fairly easy to devise a procedure whereby the Congress can say, in fiscal year 1974, the spending ceiling will be $269 billion. If, however, procedures remain as they are now, so that thirty or forty different committees in each house of the Congress go their separate ways—in social security, in veterans pensions, in disaster relief, in appropriations actions—and take individual actions whose spending consequences are $279 billion, then Congress will have abdicated to the President the entire control over spending. That is because with one vote it has said, Mr. President, you can spend only $269 billion, but with another series of about 250 votes, it has said, here are individual actions which total $279 billion and it is up to you, Mr. President, to cut that extra $10 billion. What an abdication of congressional power this would be!

But the implications are even more far-reaching. Imagine over the years a situation in which the Congress takes a cheap economy vote. Everybody can vote for an overall spending ceiling and make it very low, because that vote does not affect any one program. Meanwhile, back at the ranch, the membership of every individual committee knows that its actions on a particular appropriation or a social security bill do not really carry any weight because Congress has abdicated to the President the difficult job of reconciling its individual actions with the overall ceiling it has set. Gradually, over the years, individual appropriations committee votes will become meaningless. It is a cheap vote for a congressman to please his constituents with individual actions and a cheap vote to set a nice low expenditure ceiling, perhaps $5 billion below the President's.

Therefore, the secret to the Congress controlling spending, in addition to taking a longer look ahead, is finding a set of what must be very complicated procedures whereby the individual actions of the individual committees somehow are reconciled with a responsible total.

I am, on the one hand, very hopeful but, on the other, just a bit pessimistic that a system of government in which there are 535 individual senators and congressmen, each responsible to his own state or district, with no party leadership tight enough to impose a kind of a party budget, can devise a set of procedures that will achieve this very difficult task. For the problem is to set a ceiling that is realistic, economically justifiable, and noninflationary and then, through a series of individual actions by individual committees and individual congressmen, arrive at that total, no more and no less.

Congressman Ullman's committee, the committee of which he is cochairman, has literally a historic job before it—both in finding a way to enact a spending ceiling and in devising procedures whereby 535 very individualistic congressmen responsible to a lot of very individualistic districts can cooperate with each other in this complex job of making the sum of the parts add up to the whole.

Part 3

Discussion

Discussion

SENATOR PROXMIRE: Dr. Schultze and Dr. McCracken have both hammered away— especially Dr. Schultze in his last remarks—at the principal point, the main part of what is going to be the difficulty of Al Ullman's committee. Al is fully aware of it and I thought he explained it quite well. A ceiling by itself is passing the buck. A ceiling isn't enough. It is just the beginning, a cheap vote that means very little.

Once we have a ceiling, we then have to persuade the various responsible committees and the Congress as a whole that that means we have to handle each of the appropriation bills so as to stay within that limitation. Some appropriations will go up, some will go down, but the net has to come out at $269 billion—or whatever the ceiling is. That is a tough part of the problem.

We learned last fall—in that almost traumatic situation where finally the President took the initiative and decided what the spending ceiling would be—that if Congress doesn't act, it doesn't mean that the chairmen of the various committees will have the power to determine spending. It means the President will have that power. He *will* impound funds —and he must, if he is going to be responsible.

I approve of what the President did last year. Whether Democrats or Republicans agree or disagree, the fact is that the President acted. He will do it in the future, he will get away with it, he will have public support for it, and he will be right in doing it. Gradually we are becoming aware of this. Interestingly, in the report prepared by Congressman Ullman's committee, thirty-five of us unanimously agreed that this has to be done, and that it will be done.

Now let me just comment briefly on some of the other points that were raised here.

Dr. Schultze said we need a three- to five-year budget—that one year isn't enough. He is absolutely right. Witnesses before the Joint Economic Committee, especially administration witnesses, must be bored with the fact that I always bring this point up. I keep asking for a five-year prediction—which they've never given us before and we have to have it. If Congress doesn't know what is going to happen, what the administration's forecast is, then it's hard for us to formulate any kind of a long-term budget. What we've brought out in this discussion so far is that when Congress acts on appropriations, it is deciding about more than one year; it is deciding for years down the pike. So it must have full awareness of what the impact is going to be in '75, '76, '77, and so forth.

I disagree with my good friend, John Byrnes from Wisconsin, on one point. I agree with about 95 percent of his presentation, but he indicated the President is holding down spending and he said, "Thank heaven he is." I couldn't disagree more. The President isn't holding down spending, John. His proposed 1974 budget is a fat budget in every sense. He has asked for a $19 billion increase in spending—7.5 percent! And, furthermore, the increase is not confined to military spending, the area which has been mainly attacked.

HUD outlays will increase 30 percent in 1974. People think that these programs, the so-called substantive human domestic programs, are going to be cut. But model cities will be up by $17 million, neighborhood facility grants by 35 percent, open space/land programs by 20 percent, and urban renewal funds by $50 million. HEW's budget won't be cut either. It's going to go up $4 billion under the Nixon spending requests. Income security—that's social security and so forth—will increase by $6 billion. Sewage plant construction—there are all kinds of complaints about how that is being cut—will be up 80 percent—80 percent! And urban mass transit is to go up 30 percent.

Now, what all this adds up to is that the President is

taking action this year that may result in somewhat lesser expenses in 1975 and '76, but what about the next few years?

Dr. Arthur Burns said recently in testimony before our committee, in 1930 all agencies of government—state, local and federal—were spending about 10 percent of our income; in 1940, they claimed 20 percent, and this year, 35 percent. I think all of us will agree that there are services only the government can perform, that they should be performed well, and that we are going to have to increase spending in some areas. But 35 percent is just too much. We have gone too far.

To make any progress with this problem, we have to reduce the rhetoric—and I hope this debate will help do that. Everybody, as has been indicated here, favors cutting spending. The President does, for example, but he just isn't doing it. We have to recognize that his fiscal 1974 budget actually describes an increase in spending right down the line.

Finally, I think that Al Ullman put his finger on something we ought to be pretty happy about: Congress at long last is beginning to develop a workable, as he put it, long-range mechanism for considering spending in a framework that will enable us to know where we are going.

I suppose the real question is, who has the power? And if Congress is going to maintain this power, then it must not only set a ceiling, but exercise the discipline and restraint and pain of saying "no" to itself in many areas.

MODERATOR GORALSKI: Congressman Ullman, you have an unusual responsibility here as cochairman of the Joint Study Committee on Budget Control. Do you have any further comments?

CONGRESSMAN ULLMAN: Last year the issue came into focus when the President proposed a spending ceiling, and a great hue and cry went up that it would be an abdication of authority, spending authority, for Congress to enact that ceiling. Congressman Byrnes and I on the Ways and

Means Committee heard a great deal of debate on that subject.

I agree that we must live within a spending ceiling. The whole problem of the dollar around the world, the great imbalance of trade, clearly points to the fact that this is no longer an optional matter. We simply must live within our means. But the problem has been that Congress has no mechanism for doing so. And that is why the study committee was set up.

Congressman Byrnes has suggested that procedural matters aren't that important. I don't agree. I think that the members of Congress are basically responsible, but we don't have the procedures that enable them to be responsible. All of the incentives are to vote for all of the spending programs —as has been pointed out here repeatedly. There are no procedures whereby we can fit the pattern together and add up the pieces into a whole. If we establish budgeting procedures that force us to fit the parts into the whole, if the members have an opportunity to vote on a budget that relates spending to revenue and to bind themselves, when they initiate a new program, to fit it into the whole pattern, then, I think, we would have the kind of responsibility the nation believes the Congress should assume.

The real answer, of course, is not just one annual spending ceiling. What we need is an annual spending ceiling projected one, two, three, four, and five years into the future. A simple one-year ceiling wouldn't handle the case where we adopt new programs that have a broadening base. Sometimes the name of the game, as has been pointed out here, is to spend just a little piece of a new program this year and project the big spending into the future. Well, if you enter into five or six such programs that balloon in that fashion, the budget is totally out of control by the time you get out there two or three years.

The whole process we are envisioning encompasses computerization. It encompasses a permanent staff with fiscal expertise whose work we can use to evaluate the national program for revenues and expenditures, and establish our own priorities within that limit. Just establishing a limit itself is not, as we pointed out, the answer at all. But a mechanism for dividing up the pie and for containing and establishing our own priorities within an outer limit is the real answer.

MR. BYRNES: First, I can't quite understand why the senator would disagree with me with respect to the President cutting spending.

What is all the howling about, senator, if the President isn't cutting back on the amount of money that is proposed to be spent—the howling about the $14 billion that he has impounded? These days I keep reading about some senator or some congressman—I don't want to be partisan about this, but most of them are of your political faith [Laughter] —raising the devil about what havoc is going to be caused by the President's cutting or impounding of these funds. Of course, that is just what happens when spending cuts are made. Somebody's favorite program is cut back and he howls.

Maybe you and I could agree, senator, that the President is not cutting enough. Certainly I am not going to let you be a greater saver than I am. [Laughter.] When I was in Congress—

SENATOR PROXMIRE: That's what I'm working on, John. [Laughter.]

MR. BYRNES: —I was accused too often, senator, of casting more no votes than yes votes.

But my point is that it is wrong to suggest the President is not cutting back. I think anybody who listens to the radio or reads the papers and magazines would find that they are complaining he is cutting too much. Now, you are welcome to your opinion that he isn't cutting enough. And I might even subscribe to that. But thank God he's doing at least as much as he is.

SENATOR PROXMIRE: What you are saying reflects the impression the President has been successful in getting across. He succeeded in this, primarily I think, because many members of Congress don't really appreciate or perhaps understand it.

The fact is that even if we—

MR. BYRNES: You don't think the impounding is saving any money?

SENATOR PROXMIRE: —restored all of the impounded funds, for the OEO and for the farm disaster program and so forth, well—we have dug around this budget and we can't find more than $3 billion to put back.

MR. BYRNES: You had better converse with some of your senators—

SENATOR PROXMIRE: I think that's why—

MR. BYRNES: —and tell them that the President really isn't being as harsh as they say he is, isn't ruining the country by trying to hold down expenditures. [Laughter.]

SENATOR PROXMIRE: We can cut the defense budget by $4 billion and just keep defense programs at their present level. The war is over. We can cut foreign aid by $1 billion. So we can cut well below the President's—

MR. BYRNES: Now you are getting into the question of what you think are the priorities.

SENATOR PROXMIRE: That's true.

MR. BYRNES: And I was talking about the total. You said he wasn't making any impact on the total.

SENATOR PROXMIRE: Well, you don't hear many speeches on the floor of the Senate that the defense budget isn't high enough.

DR. SCHULTZE: Can a layman get into this? [Laughter.]

In part, what is happening this year with the President's budget for 1974 illustrates the tragedy of the lack of procedures for enabling the Congress to come up with an alternative. If you took a poll of fiscal experts—don't ask me to define a fiscal expert [Laughter] —I would think 95 percent of them would agree that the President's total spending is not too low, and most of them would agree it is not too high either.

The real problem is that many people think it's the right total but the wrong set of priorities, as I happen to do. For example, if you look in *The Budget of the United States Government, Fiscal Year 1974* (page 57), he projects expenditure cuts of $17 billion in 1974 and $22 billion in 1975, of which—see page 52—only $2.7 billion or a little more than 10 percent comes out of the defense budget and all the rest out of the domestic budget, and if you look at the fact that the budget doesn't touch the tax code and all the loopholes in it, you can see there is a real honest-to-God, legitimate debate between liberals and conservatives on priorities. Most people would agree on the size of the pie but disagree on how it should be split.

As far as I know, there is no way the voters are going to be able to get their hands on that debate. How do we shift funds out of the loopholes in the tax code, and to some extent out of the defense budget, into more rewarding programs—"more rewarding" being my definition. That way we can't find.

And here again, I would hope that Congressman Ullman's committee will come up with a procedure whereby Congress not only decides about totals, how to hold down spending— which, in my view, is not the big controversy—but where the spending should be put. I don't really know any way to do this.

SENATOR PROXMIRE: That is exactly where the public focus is, as John Byrnes has indicated. The people think that Congress is spending money endlessly and that the

President is the hero because he is fighting to hold it down. This is baloney. There is probably no real difference between Republicans and Democrats on the ceiling. I would like to see it lower. Some might want it a little higher. But I think you could get a majority of Democrats to agree we shouldn't go over $268.7 billion.

But the rhetoric sounds as if the Democrats want to spend another $10 billion. I don't think they do.

MR. BYRNES: But, senator, I think everybody agrees that one of the things Congress has to look at is the total.

SENATOR PROXMIRE: That's right.

MR. BYRNES: And the total that Congress had appropriated for fiscal 1973, or the total that would have been projected for fiscal '74, was too big. So the President has cut it back down.

Now, sure, we can disagree on our priorities. And that, as I have suggested, is one of the difficult parts of the problem. Economy is fine—we can all agree about it—if it's on the other guy's projects. But the total—that is one of the big difficulties. And you, Al and the rest have my greatest sympathy—in trying to establish a way in which Congress can make a reasonable determination as to what are the priorities. As things stand now, Congress never addresses itself to that point, really.

DR. McCRACKEN: Of course, the questions about the total and the questions of priorities are interdependent and interrelated precisely because, in general, we can all solve our priority problem by adding more to the total. But the trouble is that then we come out with a total nobody wants. So these two things are very close.

I think that without a more explicit procedure for focusing on the total, we cannot really get at the priority question.

CONGRESSMAN ULLMAN: That is why, though, we are never really going to face up to the issue of impoundment until Congress itself devises a system of determining the priorities. This is the number one objective of the budget study committee. The second one is to put an outer limit on expenditures. The two have to go together.

SENATOR PROXMIRE: Let me just respond to that point, Al, by saying that if we set the ceiling first, as you proposed in your statement, the impoundment issue disappears, because then the President loses the argument of fiscal responsibility, of keeping taxes down and beating inflation. Then, within that ceiling of, say, $268.7 billion—within that, we can decide where the spending is and Congress should prevail—

CONGRESSMAN ULLMAN: But it is only effective if Congress sets a limit on itself and then divides up the pie itself.

SENATOR PROXMIRE: That's right.

CONGRESSMAN ULLMAN: In other words, we devise a system of determining our own priorities and stay within the outer limits. Then the issue of impoundment is dead—

SENATOR PROXMIRE: Right.

CONGRESSMAN ULLMAN: —because we would have committed ourselves to the right amount of spending for the economy in a given situation, because we would have divided it up, because we would have eliminated the pipeline. Therefore the President, in order to spend the right amount for the economy, would have to spend it in the places that the Congress directs.

MODERATOR GORALSKI: Thank you, gentlemen. We will now take questions from the guests here at our Town Hall Meeting.

JOHN KOLE, *Milwaukee Journal:* Could we have some discussion from the other panel members on Mr. Schultze's comments about priorities, especially on two points: First, should domestic spending for the various HEW programs and housing programs be cut or expanded? And, second, what about tax loopholes? Is it feasible to think that considerably more money can be gotten from this approach?

CONGRESSMAN ULLMAN: Let me address myself briefly to the tax situation, and I think Congressman Byrnes will probably bear me out.

There certainly are tax loopholes that need to be plugged, and right now in the Committee on Ways and Means we are engaged in extensive hearings on that subject. We intend to produce a tax bill that plugs just about every loophole we can find. But, unfortunately, any tax bill that can pass the Congress is likely to include a lot of reforms that cost money. If single people are to be treated equitably, it will cost maybe $6 or $7 billion. Or if the poorer people are to receive additional relief from taxes, that will cost another $6 or $8 or $10 billion.

So it seems to me that whatever revenues we pick up by plugging loopholes for corporations or for the rich, we are likely to spend by giving tax relief to others. In the long run, the only real way to gain more tax revenues is to make the tax code more equitable and then raise the rates. I think that we are going to come out with a program that will be pretty well balanced. It will be a tax reform bill and a good one. But it is not going to produce a lot of revenue.

MR. BYRNES: Jack, I can understand what prompts your question, but it seems to me that the problem of how to decide what are the proper priorities is a whole other program. One of the difficulties that is involved, as I tried to point out, in the process of controlling spending is how to get 535 members of Congress as a group—a majority of them—to agree as to the proper distribution of spending, the proper priorities. And that is one of the difficulties that led to the present situation, it seems to me, where Congress has abdicated its power to such a large degree to the President. Somebody has to have the guts to say no to one program, to say yes to another and to modify the third.

It seems to me that the question we have before us today is how to develop the system that leads to a majority consensus in keeping with the needs of the country as to what the division of this pie, if you want to use that phrase, should be.

SENATOR PROXMIRE: Let me be very specific, Jack, in answering your questions.

As you know, I have suggested a counterbudget. But I think we can make a strong economic argument for increasing some of the human resources programs because they are antiinflationary. Manpower training provides skills for people who lack a skill now. Programs in this area can lessen the pressures of scarce skilled labor if they are operated properly. But manpower training is being reduced, and it shouldn't be.

Second, we can provide funds for farm disaster relief in areas—like some in Wisconsin, and I'm sure it's true elsewhere throughout the country—where farmers are simply going to have to let their farms go because they don't have the funds they thought were promised them. That would mean less food production, and therefore higher food prices. So if we provide these funds, it will help hold down food prices.

And, third, take the housing programs, which have a long-range effect. As I pointed out, the increase in HUD expenditures for fiscal 1974 is going to be about 30 percent. But by 1975 there will be much less in the pipeline for low- and moderate-income housing. What that means, of course, is that the vacancy rate, which is very low now, will be so squeezed that rents will skyrocket and inflation will be much more serious.

These are three programs that should be funded for modest sums, and I am sure we can fund them and other programs that really have merit and still come in under the President's budget.

Now, as to the question on tax loopholes, I would agree that we can raise at least $5 billion, perhaps $10 billion, by plugging loopholes so as to have greater equity in the tax structure. But I don't think it makes sense now, under present circumstances, to turn around and spend that money. It should be used instead to achieve a more equitable tax structure. Today a very large proportion of our tax revenues comes from payroll taxes, which are highly regressive. The additional revenues we get from plugging tax loopholes should go toward easing that burden.

RICHARD P. NATHAN, Brookings Institution: There has been a lot of agreement among the panel members about goals, but they seem quite vague on how to actually achieve them. Congressman Ullman spoke about needing a mechanism for dividing up the pie and getting the Congress to stick to component sub-ceilings of an overall ceiling. How precisely can the Congress make this happen? How would it operate?

MODERATOR GORALSKI: Dr. McCracken, do you want to respond first to Mr. Nathan's question of how to divvy up the pie?

DR. McCRACKEN: I take it the chairman wants the member of the panel who is least impeded by any practical experience to comment on this. [Laughter.]

Let me make just one or two general comments of principle. First, I should think this problem will be one of the most difficult that the joint study committee is going to have to come to grips with. One thing, however, we need to bear in mind is that this is not only an extremely sensitive issue, but also an extraordinarily complex one. I think "we"—that is, the citizenry—must be realistic in our expectations. The important thing, it seems to me, is that this effort to control spending gives some evidence of coming to grips with what has been almost a total absence of a structure for engendering the discipline that has tended to fade out of budgetry in the last thirty years—namely, the discipline that comes from budgeting against a total.

Whatever procedure is chosen, I am sure it will be unsatisfactory the first time around or even the tenth time around. The question is, can we make some progress?

Second—to use the phrase which Congressman Byrnes questions, dividing up the pie—we need to bear in mind that the priorities we are talking about here are not just how to divide up the pie that we call a budget. They also involve how to divide up a pie which is the larger pie of our total economic capability. In other words, the pie here is really gross national product, not just the budget—particularly when the total budget, including federal, state and local outlays, has reached the point where it is 40 percent or thereabouts of the total national income.

SENATOR PROXMIRE: The answer is partly being worked out now. Chairman McClellan of the Senate Appropriations Committee has asked every subcommittee chairman to estimate how low he thinks he can hold his subcommittee spending for this year. I have filed my estimates, and so have other chairmen. Senator McClellan is working on them.

Now, we may not be able to stay within these estimates, but it is a beginning. First we will have to try to get the subcommittee to go along. Some subcommittees may come out above their estimates; some may even be below. Then we have to go to the floor, of course. This is a long, tough, hard, painful process in which there is going to be all kinds of give-and-take. But I think it is very healthy. As Dr. McCracken said, it is going to mean that for the first time we will be trying to budget against a specific limit. And we do have the President's budget as the framework within which to work. I think that is very helpful.

MR. BYRNES: On this point, though, shouldn't Congress look at an expenditure budget, not just an obligational authority budget? Today it doesn't look at the expenditure side at all as far as any given year is concerned. And it should even go back into the authorizations, because of the back-door spending. There are a lot of other complications in this, as Dr. McCracken pointed out.

But the first thing is to have Congress give some attention to the expenditure budget as presented by the President. As I suggested in my earlier remarks, individual congressmen now make speeches about spending, as the senator is doing now. But Congress itself doesn't address itself to that aspect at all. It addresses itself, Charlie, as you know, to new obligational authority—which is way down the line and has only a partial impact on what the spending level will be this fiscal year and therefore what it will be next fiscal year and the next.

CONGRESSMAN ULLMAN: Something that hasn't been stressed enough is the fact that only 44 percent of the budget is controlled by the appropriations committees. And legislative committees don't deal in annual expenditures. They deal in obligational authority for programs extending over a period of years.

So the first task for a congressional budget committee would be to move into the legislative appropriating area, the backdoor spending area, and to recommend priority allocations—with the advice and consent of the various legislative committees, of course. Then it should do the same to the appropriations committees, asking them to divide up their own pie.

One of the main mechanisms we would suggest after the initial recommendations have beeen made is a wrap-up appropriations bill toward the end of each session. The budget committee would come back to the appropriations committees with revised expenditure and revenue recommendations based on the latest picture of the economy, after consultation with the Joint Economic Committee and other sources. Then the appropriations committees would rework the various appropriations bills to comply with that overall framework.

In other words, out of this would come a semblance of one unified budget. But it would come toward the end of the process, after we had acted individually, through a revision of the previous actions. This would be the practical way of implementing priorities in the Congress.

SENATOR PROXMIRE: One more comment, because I think this is so complicated. We have to operate at several levels. We have to operate on an intermediate-term basis for several years; and we also have to operate for the next year, cutting off outlays at a certain point. And the latter might be a little easier than you think for the Congress, because what will be involved will be not our appropriations process, but rather putting a ceiling on defense spending, a ceiling on space spending, a ceiling in the housing area, and so forth— *for outlays.*

I think this can be accomplished. But of course it relates, first, to trying to find out what the various subcommittee chairmen think and then to trying to work it through the will of the Congress as a whole.

ATTIAT OTT, Clark University: My question is addressed to the panel and in particular those who represent us in Congress.

It seems to me that for a long time Congress has had a set of priorities which reflect mostly the views of committees and lobbyist groups, and very little the views of the public that has to pay. Isn't it about time something quite different should be done, such as national referenda on priorities? Why not put alternative priorities to the public, to the little man who is supposed to pay for these priorities?

SENATOR PROXMIRE: That is what members of Congress are elected to do, of course. We kind of pass the buck when we ask for a referendum.

The referendum would have to be so complicated. And there would be all kinds of lobbying and people could get confused. Out in California they have referenda of the kind you are suggesting. In the recent election, there were something like sixty issues to vote on. The ballot was that long.

There is some merit, however, in the kind of questioning done by both Gallup and Harris. Harris recently had a referendum on various programs which delighted me because it indicated the public wanted both the cuts and increased expenditures to be where I thought they ought to be. But I don't think a formal national referendum with millions of people voting is practical. There just wouldn't be time for it. It would be subject to enormous oversimplification and distortion. There's really no alternative to the members of Congress stepping in and biting the bullet. We were elected to do that, and we can't pass it on.

CONGRESSMAN ULLMAN: Senator, in addition to that, if we had a mechanism for facing up to priorities—in other words, if we had a wrap-up appropriation bill where we had to decide whether we wanted the money to go to the military or to HEW—that would focus the issue for the public.

The fact that we never face up to either/or issues in spending, that we don't have any procedures for determining priorities, simply means that the public doesn't focus on the issue at all. But if we had the procedures, I think we would get a reading from the public.

PROFESSOR OTT: But I still think that Congress is failing to perform its duty. It does not make the economic issues public. When it examines appropriations, how many of the public come to listen? Only lobbyist groups, special interests. Who would be willing to pay his way to Washington to testify or listen to what you are doing? You still have to devise a procedure somehow by which you get an input. And the public doesn't elect you because of your views on economic issues at all. They elect you for a lot of other things besides how you are going to vote on national issues.

MR. BYRNES: It isn't just a matter of lobbyists and the pressure of lobbies. The way Congress is organized everything is segmentalized, and I guess that is how it must be, given the volume of work before the Congress. No small group can encompass the whole thing, so the work is divided up. And then each division, all of the authorizing committees, has its particular little area of jurisdiction which becomes its private province. Understandably, these committees develop a special sympathy for their particular area, an allegiance to doing good for the areas in their jurisdiction, and without reference to the whole.

What Congressman Ullman is talking about is the necessity of having one place of authority on overall budget questions. The biggest problem will be defining the place of authority that then takes all of these narrower jurisdictional decisions and says, no, you have gone hog wild on this one—or, maybe you haven't done enough in this area. But mostly it will be that they have all gone a little too far—and not that very many of them will have done too little for the areas in their province.

And then, after establishing that central point, the next problem will be getting the majority of the Congress to agree that the priorities established by that group are acceptable. To visualize this, all one has to do is imagine the conflicts that would occur if the senator and I, or any other two of us here tonight, got into a discussion of priorities. We would all come up, I am afraid, with a different batch. The difficult task is to bring it all together and get a majority.

DR. McCRACKEN: I have a certain amount of sympathy with what Mrs. Ott has said. Her concern is germane in this matter of trying to give some consideration to the total. And it comes back to the point that I alluded to a few minutes ago, that the pie we are dividing up is, in the final analysis, not some disembodied budget. In the final analysis we are quarreling about the total national income. Because if the process tends to enlarge the budget, then, of course, that is also a priority decision.

Now, one of the questions here is, or ought to be, this: Is

there some way by which it would be possible to get some input about the profile of the general public's preferences, as it were—which may not be expressed, or at least expressed in a highly focused way, in the normal course of the congressional procedure. I think that is what she is getting at, and she has an important point.

ELMER STAATS, General Accounting Office: I have a related question, which has to do with the realism of establishing a ceiling and overall priorities if the public does not have some opportunity to participate in the establishment of that ceiling.

Mr. Schultze has referred to the question of how the public gets in on the debate about priorities. Congressman Byrnes has referred to the need for public support. Senator Proxmire has also referred to the absence of a public viewpoint in the hearings. My question to Congressman Ullman and Senator Proxmire is this: Why would it not be feasible to have a limited number of hearings at which members of the public could make their presentations, not on minor projects, but in terms of the overall thrust of defense versus nondefense or new taxes versus a lower ceiling. Why not have them speak to issues of this type before the Congress commits itself?

My reason, in part, for raising this question is that it may not be realistic for the Congress to attempt to establish a ceiling, if it is to be meaningful, unless there is some opportunity for the public to express its views about that ceiling.

SENATOR PROXMIRE: I think we should do it. It is an excellent idea, and we need that kind of input. But I think, number one, we would have a timing problem. We would have to do all these things rather quickly, because unless we arrive at a ceiling very early in the session, we would have lost the ball game.

What I quarrel with you about on this, Elmer, is the word public. If by public you mean somehow to get the pulse of what everybody in the country thinks, I think you are lost. If you are talking about noncongressional or nonexecutive branch people—nongovernment people, if you will, experts from the universities, from Brookings, from these other institutions whose personnel have a particular competence and can contribute a more objective view than members of either Congress or the Executive Branch—marvelous! I think that would be very helpful. We need it, and we ought to have it.

But as far as the general public is concerned, I am lost as to who represents the general public if Congress and the President don't.

DR. SCHULTZE: I think it should be stressed that the way Congress sets up its procedures tends to determine a good part of the political life of the nation and specifically what issues get debated. There are some 1,500 different appropriations, I believe, with a $268 billion budget; each of the appropriations has many different categories. You can't get a public view on that. But if the Congress had procedures like those Congressman Ullman is suggesting—in other words, if at some stage of the game there was an explicit debate about shifting money from, say, defense to nondefense or health to education—I think what would begin to happen would be something like this: The Democratic Study Group would come out with its own rough budget; the Republicans' Wednesday Club would also produce a general statement. Hopefully, five or six alternative budget structures would be offered, which would then be debated in the Congress.

I don't really think that public hearings or referenda are so important. What is important is that this complex reality gets boiled down into four, five or six broad alternatives that the papers then begin to write about, that the lobbyists—and lobbyists is a good term in many cases—testify about, and that the columnists analyze in the Sunday supplements. Right now there is no simplification; there is no way to get public debate about choices because it is just too darned complex.

But priority-setting, which involves the making of broad choices, would begin to generate the kind of debates in Congress, the kind of counter-budgets from interested groups, that just might in turn generate public discussion and controversy about what is going on.

DAVID MEISELMAN, Virginia Polytechnic Institute: I would like to suggest a proposal and ask Senator Proxmire what his view would be of this:

My proposal is to have taxpayers earmark their taxes. Essentially, there should be some plan on the income tax return where taxpayers could specify how their taxes would be spent and whether they wanted more expenditures and correspondingly higher taxes or fewer expenditures and lower taxes. Rather than have debates, which, it seems to me, are the province of professional debaters and people like ourselves, something along these lines might give ordinary taxpayers a chance to exercise their choice.

SENATOR PROXMIRE: Well, that's fascinating. But what would happen to the poverty programs? So many people, poor people, don't have an income and wouldn't file an income tax, or wouldn't respond on it, that they would be underrepresented. The people who would vote would be the taxpayers. And they should vote, should have a lot to say about what happens to their money. It would be a helpful thing, but I don't think it should be governing because it has limitations.

Moreover, while it's an interesting idea, I'd want to see first how something we are currently trying works out. Beginning with the 1972 income tax returns, there is a little box which enables people, if they wish to do so, to contribute a dollar to the Republican or Democratic party. I understand that the box has been successfully hidden by the IRS so that very few people can find it, and only 4 percent have used it so far. [Laughter.]

If we don't get much participation in this scheme, I think maybe your suggestion wouldn't be very fruitful either. But I see nothing wrong with it, provided, however, that we kept it in perspective and recognized the results weren't the vote of all the people, just of those rich enough to pay taxes.

MICHAEL A. FORGASH, staff of Representative Elford A. Cederberg, Michigan: Would the congressional members of the panel address the problem of timing? As you know, the current procedure of coterminous authorizing and appropriating creates some acute difficulties. I would like to hear comment on calendar-year appropriations or whatever solutions you see for avoiding the problem of coming up to September without an education bill.

SENATOR PROXMIRE: Could I start on that, because I thought about it very hard just today when Dr. Burns testified before the Joint Committee on Budget Control. He suggested June 30 as the date for the ceiling. That is much, *much* too late. If we wait until June 30, action will have already been taken on some appropriations bills in one house or the other. Those appropriations will have been formulated without reference to a ceiling, without being subject to the discipline of an overall ceiling or a specific ceiling. There might, therefore, even be kind of a rush to get your appropriation bill in a little early.

After June 30 we begin to have to operate on continuing resolutions—which is very bad and which means that the Congress has already started to lose control, and that the executive can step right in—indeed has to. So I would say that March 15 is about the latest date for adopting a ceiling. We can't act by that date this year, of course, but I would hope we could act shortly after that.

Frankly, I am going to offer an amendment on the floor of the Senate within the next week for a ceiling of $265 billion. I don't expect to win on it. But I hope we will debate it and get an opportunity to act on it. And I am going to keep hammering away at this so that members of the Senate have this kind of opportunity to operate. They can vote against economy many times if they want to, but eventually they are going to have to come to a vote on it. And the sooner, the better.

MR. FORGASH: But do you think the period between March 15 and June 30 is long enough to deal with both the authorizations process and the appropriations process?

SENATOR PROXMIRE: Well, it's tough. I don't think we can set an earlier date than that right now. Maybe we can back it up a little. But if we get it to March 15, we would be doing mighty well. This whole thing is going to be uncomfortable and difficult. But I would like to see us at least start on it.

CONGRESSMAN ULLMAN: Let me add, senator, that one of the interim recommendations of the study committee —and I want to commend the interim report because it lays out some of these proposals in detail—is that we project the authorizing process one year ahead. I think this has to be done—

SENATOR PROXMIRE: Yes.

CONGRESSMAN ULLMAN: —if we are going to be responsible. Many people don't realize that one of the reasons the appropriations committees are so slow is that they can't act until they receive authorizing legislation from the legislative committees. In a number of cases, for instance, the Senate Appropriations Committee has not received the authorization legislation, and therefore we haven't been able to appropriate. The study committee expects to recommend year-in-advance authorization by the legislative committees.

PETER GALL, *Business Week:* Isn't it a bit unrealistic to say that by taking the fiscal argument away from the President, impoundment will be stopped? Once Congress has had the guts to say no, once it has set its priorities, once it has come up with something within a framework, what is to keep the President from impounding anyway—from using the budget as a political document, which it has always been, as much as a spending document?

SENATOR PROXMIRE: He is going to impound.

MR. GALL: Isn't Congress going to ask from him some understanding that if it does its thing, he will not impound?

SENATOR PROXMIRE: Well, frankly, I am not sure that some degree of impounding isn't necessary at all times. I can recall back in 1962 when I offered an amendment to knock $10 billion out of the budget for an additional wing of B52 bombers. My amendment got exactly four votes in the Senate. I was supporting President Kennedy when I offered my amendment, so that vote showed the power of the President and myself. At any rate, that appropriation was in the law, and the President seemingly was required to spend the money. But he decided he wouldn't. He impounded the money instead. I thought the President was right, and nobody complained.

There is always going to be some stretching out of program spending. What we object to, however, is killing an entire program. I think that sort of thing will be much harder for the President to sustain, in his relations with the Congress and the public, than a stretch-out.

CONGRESSMAN ULLMAN: Let me add this: If, for instance, $260 billion is the right amount of expenditures for a given economic situation, and if Congress has an expenditure ceiling and apportions expenditures in line with its own priorities, and if the President can't spend beyond the limits that Congress has imposed in the different priority areas—and if this whole thing adds up to $260 billion—then I think it is very unlikely the President would reduce any of those expenditures, because he would be reducing the total spending required to keep the economy moving.

DAVID BARNETT, *Hearst Newspapers:* I recall that Dr. Schultze was the director of the Bureau of the Budget during those past cases of impoundment. Do you find that the impounding this year is quite different from what it was in the years when you were director?

DR. SCHULTZE: Yes, I think it is, without assessing right or wrong.

In the past there was always a nice healthy ambiguity about the President's right to impound and what he could and couldn't do. In most periods in the past, activist Presidents wanted something out of Congress. So when they impounded, they were kind of careful and there was negotiation back and forth. If Congress screamed too loud, they let a little bit go. It sounds sloppy, but it was a nice, healthy balance of power.

This President has a much tougher budget problem. And, secondly, he doesn't want anything from the Congress. As a consequence, he can well afford to thumb his nose at every appropriation committee chairman because he doesn't care, he doesn't want anything from him. Thus there is a difference, a substantial difference, in degree and in ultimate impact. Even though most Presidents have impounded, they have done it in kind of a negotiating relationship with the Congress. But today it is pretty much absolute and flat.

SENATOR PROXMIRE: Charlie, I disagree with you that President Nixon doesn't want something from Congress. I think he is going to want some military spending from the Congress that he probably won't get. He is going to want aid for North Vietnam and he is not going to get that. And he is going to want other foreign aid money, which he is unlikely to get.

I think that every President, including President Nixon, has to be dependent on Congress to a considerable extent.

DR. McCRACKEN: It seems to me the major difference between present and past cases of impoundment is not so much one of principle as one of amounts.

BRUCE F. DAVIES, Georgetown University: Nothing has

been said so far about the implications of the proposals being considered here for fiscal policy. I would like to ask Dr. Schultze and Dr. McCracken—given their experience in trying to produce plans and procedures that would lead to full employment without too much inflation—to discuss some of these implications.

DR. SCHULTZE: I'm not sure I know how to respond.

I guess my basic proposition would be that the fundamental problem of using fiscal policy to affect the economy has to do with budget totals, that the composition of spending is important for that purpose but not terribly important. It is really the total revenues and the total expenditures that count.

Off hand, I see nothing in improving congressional procedures for getting a handle on the budget total that would make the job of dealing with fiscal policy more difficult. And I suspect in the long run it might make it somewhat more rational and somewhat easier for the President and the Congress to work together in the right direction. This is not to say that there wouldn't be a lot of other problems that we haven't even talked about at all, problems which have to do with the relationship of fiscal policy to the economy. But so far as these procedures are concerned, I don't think they would hurt and I do think they might moderately help in that particular aspect.

DR. McCRACKEN: It seems to me quite clear theoretically that this kind of procedure might tend to decrease flexibility in the use of fiscal policy for compensatory purposes.

On the other hand, it may be that what we are seeing here is, in a sense, the completion of the fiscal revolution which began some decades ago with the development of the concept of compensatory fiscal policy. As that revolution developed, the basic concept of fiscal discipline tended to fade out of the picture a little. What seems to be involved now is that —without in any sense throwing in the towel on compensatory fiscal policy, which on the whole has worked fairly well—we are trying to see if there isn't some way to produce a little better balance in terms of fiscal discipline.

MARK NEUBAUER, Medill News Service: All of you gentlemen have stressed the need for discipline in Congress, the need to say no to special interest groups. But you have been very vague as to how to enforce that discipline. Doesn't the very power base of Congress, a power base grounded upon small geographic areas each with its own specific interests, preclude that type of discipline? For example, Senator Proxmire, could you conceivably support major cuts in dairy programs, such as dairy price supports, and still hope to maintain your position in the dairy state of Wisconsin?

SENATOR PROXMIRE: Well, the answer, of course, is that spending for the dairy industry is very healthy and constructive. [Laughter.] We will all have to admit that.

But the fact is I have only one vote. Many members of Congress feel that their constituencies deserve a champion, deserve somebody to stand up and speak for them. Each of them would reconcile this, however, in the votes of their constituents. I don't think that the special interest factor, which is a very real factor and one to be reckoned with, could be a problem unless you had a constituency that had the majority of members of the House and Senate as its champion. Then maybe you'd be in trouble. But most of these interests, whether it is oil or dairy or whatever, have limited minorities within the Congress. You just have to reconcile them, and you can, simply by majority vote.

CONGRESSMAN ULLMAN: In addition, senator, the percentage of spending that is directly associated with the special, congressional district problems is very, very minor. Most of our spending decisions in the Congress are—and have to be—broad-based. We are representatives of the whole nation. Most of the decisions we make are not related directly to any special interests in our districts at all. Certainly that is a consideration, but in the total budget picture, its effect is very, very minor.

DAVID O'NEILL, American Enterprise Institute: Congressman, there is another facet of the special interest problem. In many programs, for example in the manpower programs, there is no geographic special interest, but there is a special interest among the staffers who get hired to run the programs. These people who make their living out of a lot of these programs form powerful special interest groups that affect the character of legislation and affect the congressman. This is really, I think, a much more pervasive phenomenon than the geographic special interests.

CONGRESSMAN ULLMAN: You're talking about self-perpetuating programs.

DR. O'NEILL: That's right.

CONGRESSMAN ULLMAN: We are always involved in that. When the Office of Economic Opportunity was eliminated, we were deluged by a lot of people who had worked for it. Not that they weren't well motivated. They knew firsthand the good that was being done and they came up to tell us about it. But they also had to have some self-interest in the continued existence of OEO.

SENATOR PROXMIRE: Incidentally, one technique that could affect that would be zero-based budgeting at least every three years on every single budget item. Senator Brock and Dr. Burns spoke about it today. This would enable us to consider, every three years, whether to throw out entire programs or an entire segment of programs. With this technique, we would begin at least to challenge the parts of entrenched bureaucracy that are no longer doing anything worth continuing.

DR. O'NEILL: But most of the information or testimony that you get comes from individuals with an interest in the programs, so you tend to hear mostly that the programs work, rather than hearing criticism.

SENATOR PROXMIRE: That is true of every program. The people who testify, as I pointed out, are almost always the champions of the program. They are dying to come in. They, or the industry that is involved, will pay for it; and the labor unions want to appear if it is going to help them.

The poor little consumer or taxpayer who has to pay for all of this isn't likely to be represented because he has a generalized interest and because it is expensive to get into the act. Congress has to find some way of inviting experts who will come in on the other side of these programs and testify against them.

CARL SHOUP, United Nations: Speaking just for myself of course, I wonder whether the budget committee that is being proposed would feel an obligation to consider possible increases in tax rates or decreases in tax rates coincidentally with its determination concerning total expenditures, so that there could be, through this committee, a true balancing of the community's needs, with either a larger part of the pie going to private spending or a larger part to government spending through changes in tax rates. And along with that, there would, I presume, have to be consultation with the Federal Reserve Board as to its policies and as to how the deficit, if any, is to be financed. Or does this kind of thing lie more or less outside the budget committee's concern as it is now being viewed?

CONGRESSMAN ULLMAN: No. In our interim report we have gone specifically to that matter. We haven't spoken about it a great deal because spending seems to be the controversial issue. But the budget committee could very definitely recommend a revenue goal to the House Ways and Means Committee and the Senate Finance Committee. The Ways and Means Committee would have to report back measures for reaching that revenue goal. Additionally, we would have to devise procedures whereby, if an amendment to an appropriation bill extended the appropriation beyond the amount specified, then either this extra funding would have to be obtained by reducing another category or there would have to be a requirement that the taxes be increased to that amount.

RONALD HOFFMAN, Council of Economic Advisers: If the Congress did have an expenditure budget of its own, would it make it easier for the Congress to give the President flexibility to change tax rates for fiscal policy purposes?

SENATOR PROXMIRE: I would very much oppose that, and I think most members of Congress would, if only because one of the very few powers we really have now is the power to determine taxes. We erode that power when we give it to the President. The flexibility argument is a pretty good argument. But a lot of people feel you can't fine-tune this economy of ours very well anyway. And once Congress surrenders and gives up the taxing power, we just don't have a great deal left. So I don't think there is much sentiment in Congress for it.

Dr. Burns has proposed flexibility for the investment credit. He wants Congress to give the President the authority to increase or decrease it. He is a very powerful man with great influence, but I don't know a single member of the Congress who supports him on that.

JERRY JASINOWSKI, Joint Economic Committee, U.S. Congress: I am struck by the immediacy of most of the questions tonight and the concentration on the spending ceiling crisis today. I am also struck by the fact that it wasn't too long ago that Charlie Schultze was telling us about the Vietnam War peace dividend. [Laughter.] Just to get a little historical perspective on what has happened between then and now, I wonder if you could tell us, Charlie, whatever happened to the peace dividend and how do we get from that to the spending ceiling issue?

DR. SCHULTZE: My recollection about what Charlie Schultze said about the peace dividend was principally that it ain't going to be there.

MR. JASINOWSKI: I guess it must have been Moynihan or someone else [Laughter]—who said there was going to be a big peace dividend. I'm sorry for being incorrect about you.

DR. SCHULTZE: Very briefly, for about 170 years of this republic, or whatever the number of years from 1789 to about 1965, it was generally true that in periods of peace-time prosperity, economic growth generated more additions to federal revenues than a normal expansion of domestic expenditures would use up. So we had a dividend every year to do new things with. For the last five to seven years, however, we have been at a point where economic growth produces an increase in federal revenues each year which is equal to or less than the expansion of the spending programs we have on the books. That gives us our problem.

How did we get that way? I think, for three reasons. First, in the last ten years the federal government has reduced its income and excise tax rates by an amount equal to $45 billion. If we had the same tax laws today we had ten years ago, we would be taking in $45 billion more this year. Second, the domestic expenditures of the federal government, which even as late as 1959 or '60 were only 6 percent of our national income, are now 13 or 14 percent, and their normal expansion takes more than it used to. And finally, Vietnam peace to the contrary notwithstanding, the defense budget is rising.

Putting all three of those things together, we are at the point where we no longer have the free gift of economic growth facing us so that we can, without raising taxes, pass out a lot of new programs. Those three things got us to where we are.

MODERATOR GORALSKI: Thank you all very much for a most stimulating discussion on the question of can Congress control spending.

Participants

DAVID L. BARNETT
News Editor
Hearst Newspapers

PHILIP COGSWELL
Washington Correspondent
Portland Oregonian

JAMES CONMY
Press Assistant
Office of Congressman Ullman

BRUCE F. DAVIE
Department of Economics
Georgetown University

JOHN FARMER
Washington Correspondent
Philadelphia Evening Bulletin

WILLIAM FELLNER
Department of Economics
Yale University
and
AEI, Resident Scholar

WILLIAM FORD
Director, Department of Research
and Planning
American Bankers Association

MICHAEL FORGASH
Administrative Aide
Office of Congressman Cederberg

HARRISON FOX
Research Director
Office of Senator Brock

PETER GALL
Washington Correspondent
Business Week

GOTTFRIED HABERLER
Resident Scholar
American Enterprise Institute

BRYCE HARLOW
Vice President, Governmental
   Affairs
Proctor & Gamble

HARLEY HENRICHS
U.S. Naval Academy

HAROLD HOCHMAN
Project Director
Public Finance Division
Urban Institute

RONALD HOFFMAN
Senior Staff Member
Council of Economic Advisers

THOMAS HUGHES
Associate Director of Economics
U.S.News & World Report

MICHAEL HUGO
Minority Clerk
House Committee on
   Appropriations

RALPH HUITT
Executive Director
National Association of State
   Universities and Land Grant
   Colleges

JERRY JASINOWSKI
Staff Economist
Joint Economic Committee

JOHN KOLE
Bureau Chief
Milwaukee Journal

ROBERT McCONNELL
Legislative Assistant
Office of Congressman Rhodes

KEITH MAINLAND
Clerk and Staff Director
House Committee on
   Appropriations

61

PARTICIPANTS

DAVID MEISELMAN
Department of Economics
Virginia Polytechnic Institute

BRUCE MEREDITH
Staff Assistant
House Committee on
    Appropriations

ALAN P. MURRAY
Vice President
First City National Bank, New
    York

RICHARD P. NATHAN
Senior Fellow
Brookings Institution

OSCAR NAUMAN
Bureau Chief
New York Journal of Commerce

DAVID O'NEILL
Director of Human Resources
    Studies
American Enterprise Institute

JUNE O'NEILL
Senior Staff Member
Council of Economic Advisers

CHARLES ORLEBEKE
Deputy Under Secretary for
    Policy Analysis and Program
    Evaluation
Department of Housing and
    Urban Development

ATTIAT F. OTT
Department of Economics
Clark University

DAVID J. OTT
Department of Economics
Clark University

GEORGE PRITTS
Legislative Assistant
Office of Senator Fannin

DEAN REED
Bureau Chief
Newhouse Newspapers

BILL ROBERTSON
Washington Correspondent
Oregon Journal

JOHN SALOMA
Department of Political Science
University of Massachusetts

CARL SHOUP
United Nations

HOWARD SHUMAN
Administrative Aide
Office of Senator Proxmire

DAVID S. SHUTE
Foley and Lardner

WILLIAM SMITH
Sutherland, Asbill and Brennan

ELMER B. STAATS
Comptroller General
General Accounting Office

ROBERT VOGEL
Senior Staff Member
Council of Economic Advisers

RICHARD WAGNER
Senior Research Staff
Urban Institute

SUSAN WAGNER
Contributing Editor
Publisher's Weekly

THELMA WHITE
Office Manager
Washington Bureau
Indianapolis Star-News

GEORGE WILL
National Review

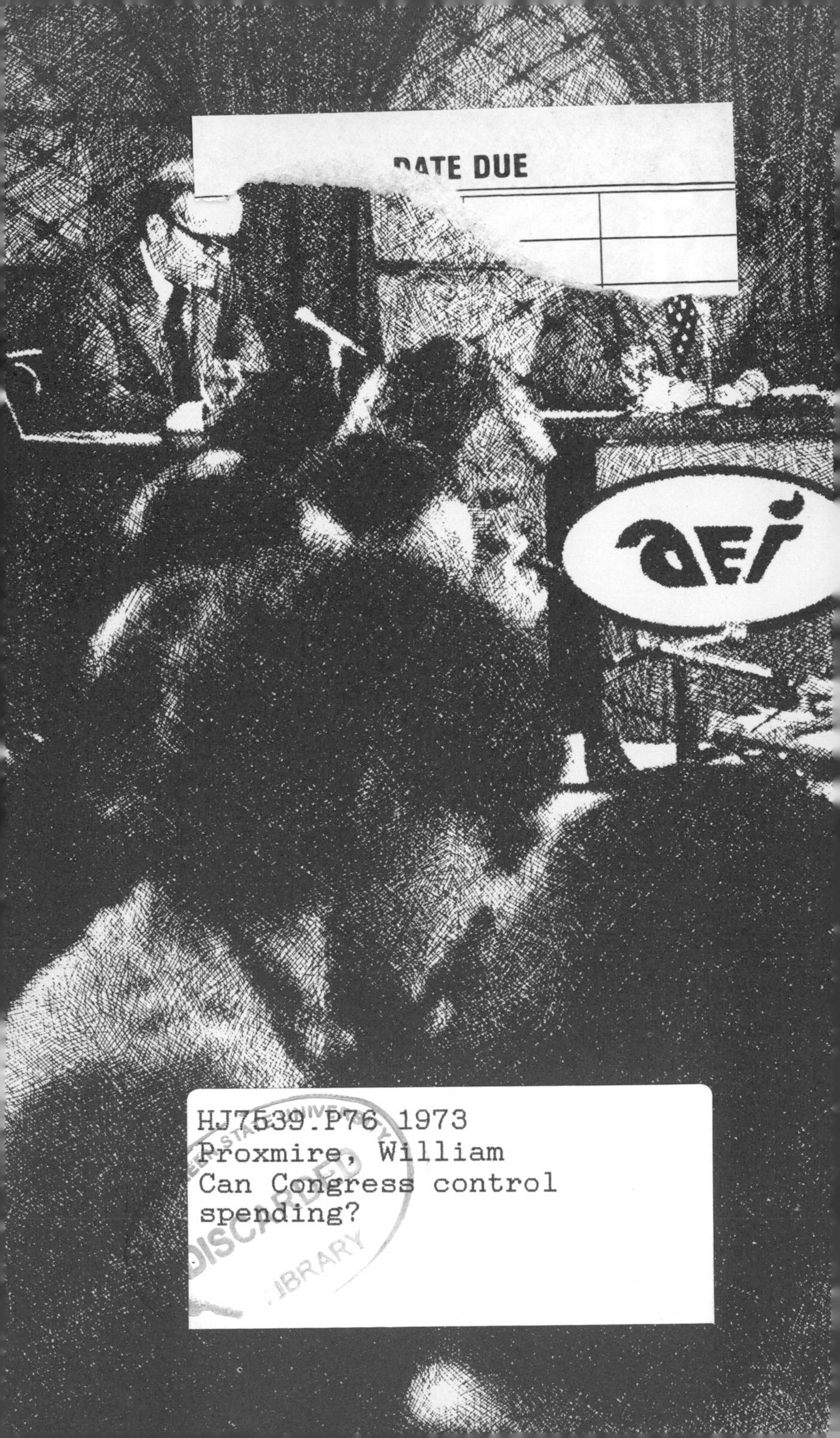